L.E.T.T.E.R.S.

T0157723

L.E.T.T.E.R.S.

Nigel Ash

authorHOUSE®

AuthorHouse™
1663 Liberty Drive
Bloomington, IN 47403
www.authorhouse.com
Phone: 1-800-839-8640

© 2012 Nigel Ash. All rights reserved.

No part of this book may be reproduced, stored in a retrieval system, or transmitted by any means without the written permission of the author.

Published by AuthorHouse   10/18/2012

ISBN: 978-1-4772-3830-1 (sc)
ISBN: 978-1-4772-3831-8 (e)

Any people depicted in stock imagery provided by Thinkstock are models, and such images are being used for illustrative purposes only. Certain stock imagery © Thinkstock.

This book is printed on acid-free paper.

Because of the dynamic nature of the Internet, any web addresses or links contained in this book may have changed since publication and may no longer be valid. The views expressed in this work are solely those of the author and do not necessarily reflect the views of the publisher, and the publisher hereby disclaims any responsibility for them.

31st July 2012 (Midnight)

My daughter tells me my writing is slurred with age.
True. I have just recalled a moment, we spent dancing
in Esher cinema's front floor, directly below screen,
watching the new S~Club movie 'Premier' exclusive
style, totally alone, on the popcorn littered floor.
Interrupted by an usherette entrance, ½ way through the
movie (spectator).

PHOTOGRAPH OF BEARER
PHOTOGRAPHIE DU TITULAIRE

Signature of bearer
Signature du titulaire

BEARER DOES NOT WRITE.

CANCELLED
CANCELLED

177, Chertsey Road
Staines.

Dearest Darling Shayla, & Daniel, 18th April 2006

Spent Easter cutting M's hedge at Dolphins SAT-MON.
Took enormous amounts of garden refuse to tip. Jumped
queue each time (legally) (Garden refuse lane empty). After each
session with the fir hedge I managed to fit in trips &
activities; SAT 15/4 I visited in the early evening a night
club bar in Windsor. It was just for a drink & free entry
(no dancing) there were an awful lot of young people
crowded around the bar with rather novel eccentric bar
inside. Half way down the bar I found an empty bar stool
with a young girl leaning on it. I asked her if she wanted
it, & she shook her head, so I sat there in my suit (no tie)
& drank my stella. People came & went, it was all very hectic.
Then two or 3 girls arrived and one accidently sat her
bottom gently on my right knee!!!!!!!!!!!!!!!!!!!!! SUN 16/4 Cycled
to Chertsey where I bought a bottle of coke and sat opposite the
church. Gave a shelf stacker in the newsagent £1 for the drink
(que barged) 10 people were queuing, didn't wait. Looked at Thorpe
Park at a distance (found a large hole in perimeter fence;
beyond the water). Was looking for fencing for M over in
Sunbury, when I found myself behind a reasonably condition
ford escort car, with two 20's year old girls with enormous

1

& powerful water pistols. They were driving at about 30MPH squirting everyone. A few odd looks from people, who thought no doubt, that it was about to rain! When we all stopped at some traffic lights, just outside Feltham, I 'flashed' them and shouted (in my car) "Come on, then" They looked back at me, but just carried on as before, squirting people. I forgot to mention, there was a man with two children, all on push-bikes. He was trying to do a "wheely", luckily he didn't fall off backwards!

MON 17/4 Finished the down hedge, at last! Drove to the Angel (where we've been with Cind) on the river at Henley-on-Thames, for a 'drink (& a drive). Had to drive extra miles as Datchet Road, NR, Windsor was closed to traffic. The outside has changed slightly. They have installed 3 enormous square canopy umbrellas, each with three "red" "night heaters" at the tops. The canopies are a lovely blue colour, and it was only half full (outside, remember) 6.45 p.m.

        Love to you all.
        Dad. Nigel X X x

I popped to St. Saviours Sunday 10AM in a white shirt & suit. A woman opened the door from inside & said to me "Waiting for your family?" I could only smile & nod.

Dearest Shayla & Daniel,   15th May 2006.
There is so much to learn, we never stop. You are young and I am
young at heart.
What a weekend!! so very busy! There are a great many new
beginnings for me. Let me tell you about the last week,
just gone. As I was on my annual holiday "working break"
I did a major service, on the old automobile: Gearbox &
engine oil changed, new oil filter(1)e spark plugs(4)
(front) I forgot about 18 months ago to lubricate new, brake pads
with special copper coloured grease (not ordinary grease
so they have been 'sticking' slightly. This means increase
unnecessary, wear, because the car is not free-wheeling
(no friction). I still have the (back) brakeshoes to do,
As I was told I am a square peg in a round hole, basicly
and have had to vacate the bungalow (converted in to a two
in Staines (near St. Bridge) 1770 Five people sharing"
storey house), pond (still kidney shaped like ours, but four
times bigger with one foot in length gold fish (e white).
The pond was originally a swimming pool, made below a
hillock, 6' high with a 4' high rockery waterfall. Amy, the
youngest daughter of three daughters, is 23 years old. She
is studying to be some sort of veterinary. She rides her
horse in Great Winsor Park, most weekends. The father had died
a few years ago. The mother (Shirley) has had breast
cancer, and treatment, she is 61, big build a little
over weight (like me, N.B. Just lost another # lbs, TOTAL LOSS OF 1½ stone so far
I am now ½ way to normal weight.) and very wise.
Amy has just sold her BMW car (personalised No. plate AMY..
for 9k. (she did not want to run two cars). I think I may have
told you about Harry, a large grey haired (short) the size of a labrador DOG &
Tigger, the cat (who looks just like Garfield, the
cartoon cat). He has lost the use of his hind legs e is
incontinent (has to wear a nappy). because of a car
accident, in the past. Both are very good natured. I did
ask Shirley if I could take Harry for a walk. But

3

Shirley was afraid he may run away from me, and get hurt (as we are near the busy "Thorpe Park" road); there are two adjoining fields, opposite the house. As there were five cars/van already parked in their drive, and was asked to leave mine in an adjoining road. I had a small box room, similar

Double Garages
mound

to yours, except one of my larger windows had a long diagonal crack in it. The windows were functional; made of wood, but not double glazed (which did not matter, because I was at the back of the house (downstairs bedroom) it was very quiet. Some guttering, overlooking the back garden was sagging badly. I mended it with two 6" nails, placed at an angle, where the old brackets for the gutter had broken. There was a square downpipe for the rain water which had become disconnected. I fixed this back together too, by laying a large 4'x4'x1" wooden board onto another single garage (in the back garden), roof baby changing mattress & roof rack. here I stored my spare car engine oil, bicycle. The Garage was rather dilapidated, (but complete) and had a very stiff, roll type, front door. Down the left hand side of the house (as you look at it) There ran, for a good seventy yards, a magnificent 18' high Bamboo 'hedge' which is 30 years old, & had grown a sort of wall of small leaves, as illustrated. Unfortunately Shirley made a bonfire in the back garden, which always permeated my closed box room windows! so sleep was in smelly air for those Tuesday nights. I'll sign off now, but I have a medium room (as 75) now, and a baby thin garden strip, full of nick nacks, and today visited by three squirrels! I know the 'enormous park' well as I have worked for Nippon Express for 4 years, as you know, recall. Nearby, someone's converted their back garden into

~ Love from Daddy

4

119
Mornington Crescent
Cranford,
Middlesex TW5 9SU

8th June 2006,

Dearest Shayla,

Do you remember Mark & Ilene Teare, from Canada? Well it's Mark's birthday today! This last week has been like a whole year, passing by in time, I have missed you all very much, especially your Wednesday & Sunday 8 P.M. calls to me. I feel the Mobile Fresh have suddenly charged me endlessly and I have lost £6 in three days!! They are a rip-off, as will explain. I have abandoned the car & it is immobilized at Dolphins, I worked an extra hour on ~~Friday 1st~~ June because I had to submit my Affidavit (sworn Bible statement) for the next court case (in July) when I will be collecting £260 stolen (by my x landlord in Egham), on Friday 2nd June morningtime. By a mistake on my part I caught an early bus from Knowle Green (law courts) to Ashford instead of Laleham. So I had my packed lunch there, on the grass green opposite your school. I saw a sign for an Open Day Fair & presumed, wrongly, that it was yours, in fact it was Spelthorne Colleges (on Sunday 4th June). As I had cycled from Cranford, hoping to see you, I went anyway. They had their local pop band, majorettes brass band playing whilst marching around the playingfield, and a series of acrobatics by gymnasts (mainly girl pupils) set to music (no singing). They were all very good. I had three attempts at "Welly" throwing (Rotaract Charity)! and won! (a beautiful big cup (29.5 metre throw!!) I christened it with some free brandy & lemonade kindly provided by a barman (I had to do a lot of begging — I had run out of money.

I spent £10.00; on a cheeseburger £2.50, a sausage roll & onions £2.00, a pint of Fosters lager, and a pint of coke, Had a lovely time altogether, Three women kissed on their cheeks (for various reasons), talked to an artist and gave the groups drummer a sip of my "cups" brandy (They are called "Loaded Dice"), near the end of the afternoon, I was so exhausted (I had been there four hours!) I found a shady spot on the far side of the field, under some large trees (with three different types of green leaves), and crashed-out (fell asleep, for 10 minutes!) Keeping a keen ear for noise (thieves after my cup?!) I am hoping to take you and Daniel out of Father's Day 18th June 2006 as discussed with Carol, last time I spoke to her (you and Daniel have missed this special day with me, for the last two years) I have cycled so much, I am a little saddle sore, as I am not used to so much exercise! I have not had a chance to weigh myself recently, but I have had to tighten my belt another knotch, Please send me a text if you are low on credit, or better still, send me another instalment of Anna Banana,

X love you X Dad X

P.S. I nearly forgot to tell you, I played football with a little boy of 3(?) and his dad, & a little girl of 5(?) and her dad, (two different occasions) with an oversized black & white plastic football, (feet & then hands) at the fair. (v. light)

119, Mornington Crescent
Cranford, Middx. TW5 9SU

Dear Shayda & Daniel.   25th June 2006,

Just a short note to announce that
there will be a fair in my local park at
Cranford on Saturday 15th July this year,

It would be lovely if you both
could come, bring some friends if you
wish, Please let me know soon. Dad.

P.T.-

7

Glastonbury was a lovely day on 17.6.06.
The journeys were about 3 hrs, both ways, but
we stopped at motorway restaurants for a break.
As I told Hazel, the outdoor service in
the ruins of the Abbey was peaceful, and
enlightening. I had taken some sandwiches
for lunch anyway, but the bishops and
other religious leaders had a magnificent
spread under tent covers. After lunch I
had a pint of Farmhouse cider 4% Alc, and
a bottle of peach beer (which was fruity &
much lighter in taste than the cider). I
took a £2 10 minute bus trip to the local
Tor, which was a 580 feet hillock with a
medieval roofless tower on top. Three
students were playing "didgeridoo" pipes (long
hollow tubes from Australia) in the tower
itself. The sounds were deep and moving
spiritualy, but not spooky! Made it back
to witness the end of another service (PM)
(of dedication), and I an ice cream before
returning in the church minibus.
Sending you both my deepest love with
a hug each. Love Dad.

ABBEY WALL WITH ARCHWAYS

½-pint
glass

old dyke
box in Pub.

Three
steps, path

eat
cone

23rd July 2006. 8pm.

What a beautiful weekend.
I spent Saturday travelling to WaxBeach Littlehampton.
Had a lovely trip A3, cut off at Guildford &
went through Horsham on A281. Lovely slow
road. X is a dream. Felt sleepy, so stopped
at a lovely farmhouse Hotel for lunch
(9 bedrooms) Wakes, Christenings & today (SAT 22/7)
a wedding reception at 3.pm. I arrived at 1pm.
Half a dozen twenty yearolds in smart emaculate
'tail' suits ̶ were having an early pre-wed
bevvy & offered me one! Me in my shorts !!
I had a fab. meal of scampi & chips + salad £7.00!
I popped accross the road (the church was opp.)
for 2.pm W. Notice my favourite hymn 412.
I tryed to sing, but I had to leave,
overcome after the first line "I'm not
going through that again", I said quietly.

9

Left for the coast and arrived about 3.30pm.
Talked for an hour whilst swimming, to
a Thailand man, whose wife appeared
later with their 3 month old baby, Grandparents
also there. Most perfect day. Arrived "home"
at 9.45pm (bike). Very emotional journey,
Music on Virgin Radio very apt, It sounds
crazy, but the lyrics were really ALIVE!
Look after my babies, I had hoped to see
them here, for their Glastonbury presents (119)

love to anyone who wants it.

Ⓓ = Dolphins.
M. = mother's (Beryl) Aunty

119, Mornington Crescent
Cranford, Middlesex
TW5 9Su.

Dearest Sheryle & Wednesday 27th September 2006.
Darling Daniel.
Sat.23,9.06 2.45pm. Took quite a while cycling
(1hr.+) to get to my final destination; Silvermere
(at the end of seven hills Rd.) Golf Club for lunch.
I asked for Lasagne but waitress lied, & said
it wasn't on the Menu, so I had scampi & chips & peas
instead, lovely! 8 month old baby girl took a
shine to me, her Lovely mum said she (the
daughter) just wanted attention, Dad & nan
were there too! friendly strangers! SUNDAY,
24, 9.06 Elisa
'looked' Glorious day, left 119 at 3.30pm for Ⓓ work
pointing old wall holes (with cement and sand mix)
Stopped off on route to M. at Waterski place (opposite
Bedfont Lakes, Ashford, Mx.). Sat on ramp (on grassbank)
Baby boy of four came a sat with me, with his mother, to watch
his dad waterski, He blew her a kiss (from the water)
but she was looking down at her son through her
silver sun glasses & missed it, but I told her as I
waved at her husband, passing by on the water!
Held momentarily trap railing A Horse & trap as
the two people sat travelling in it, (after mini
bridge (where lady in small car stopped-If you
P.T.O,

remember (large sheet of plastic lay in the road) and I honked my horn at her — you and Daniel were passengers in mum's Blue Rover (behind my old red Triumph)) going to Laleham) on the road opposite Fordbridge Park (where we all played Bowles once, and crazy golf several times). It was a free ride for about five seconds ((magical) the single horse yanked my bicycle forward three times, at about 14 miles per hour. Exciting but a little daring. That's life!

Hope to see you all soon.

B positive.   I love you.

God bless,

Nigel. (your father.)

PS.

I do hope Carol has had the boiler serviced by Gordon Jenkins; or someone. It has been two years now, and with Winter approaching it would be prudent (wise) to invest in maintainance

Loved

MK. N.D. ASh,
119, Mornington Crescent,
Cranford, Middx. TW5 9SU
29th September 2006,

Dear owner,

I write to you in the hope of renting Jasmine Cottage (Teare) in the summer of 2007. My Aunt Mary, who lived in Forearth Road, Selsdon, (near Croydon) who originally inherited Jasmine Cottage, and leased my mother and I, (plus our cousins) the cottage throughout my childhood (from 1961). I saw the Wey river flood the church, at the base of Spicer's Lane, till in '62. from the upstairs window (I had a habbit of sitting 'in' window sills and watching the world go by!) The priest came out in knee deep water, wanting some help.

I remember the luxary of the indoor wood paneled loo, and no hot water, but a tub in the kitchen, as a substitute bath,

The fireplace in the living room, for warth & drying clothes if it rained. I loved the cottage for its 4' thick walls, the narrow twisting staircase, and the "bottle" windows in the smaller room, and of course the thatched roof. The Garden at the back always full of flowers.

The stories of my great grandfather Berry (his tombstone is part of the church's path (outside). He was a doctor I believe, and his horse was spooked in the cobbled courtyard at the top of the lane where the arched passageway runs to the butcher's shop in the main square at the top of the village, outside the church grounds.

I adored the smell of baking bread. from the Bakers (one of two, now gone) which was situated above the full size picture of Dr Payne the Cornish giant, who died in the local pub, and because of his large size (you probably already know all this!) the funeral people had to cut a hole through the ceiling to lower him down (too big for the tiny staircase!)

I used to cycle to the beaches of Bude 2 miles away.

Walking the coastal foot paths, and miles of golden sands, Nets in the rock pools at low tide, and swimming in the pool below the cliffs, which I imagine is still covered at high tide.

The tea house, nearby, for strawberries and cream,

Ordering a crab, at the local butchers in the square (now gone). in Stratton

Drawing the "canal" which runs the length of the Bude beach, up to the lock, and a vague recollection of the old cinema, at the top of the town.

I have two children 13 and 17, but my aunt Mary Teare died, before we had a chance to holiday. I named my daughter's (second name) Jasmine, after the cottage, because of the wonderful holidays experienced.

Does the pub still have folk evenings? I rember "Have you seen the streets of London" song by Ralph McTell, being requisitioned many times.

God bless anyway,

Nigel

119, Mornington Crescent
Cranford
Middlesex TW5 9SW
28th November 2006,

Dear Mrs. Osmond,
Thank you for notifying me of potential
Redundancy.
I have considered this matter thoroughly
and I would like to take the opportunity of
expressing my gratitude to the Company for
their hospitality over the last two difficult
years of my life.
This is to confirm my absence on the said
31st March 2007, and accepting your redundancy
package of £2175.00 + 1 months salary.
I wish you all success in your new
premises

love Nigel.

Nigel
119, Marriage Crescent
Crawford Me 7xr 7za

My Dearest Son,

   Although I do not know any details
of your studies, I know you are working very
hard and I am very proud of you, even from
the beginning (when you first held Shayla in
your arms. I wish you well on your test
(this is for it)).

   Awkward weekend 30.12.2006 : Both
bicycle tyres replaced & one inner tube, one
inner tube repaired & brake block also replaced.
6th January 2007 (Sat) Cycled in search of a
lunch venue. Asked for a chinese from a
stranger about to get into a 'flash' car (silver)
and there it was, opposite me!! This took
place near Osterley Park (one of my whimsical
posh thoughts!) Its called "The Cottage" and
I was waited on hand & foot, lovely!!

pretty Japanese girl too (just finishing her shift).
(No one else in this fabulous restaurant —
at 2pm). But had to brave the downpour
home (½ hour ride): socks got soaked!!

Love you always,

Phil x

Darling Daughter,   Sunday 7th January 2007.

Black is not a safe colour, but if
this is your hearts desire, then so be it.
Here is the deposit I promised, so choose
wisely, and remind me nearer May for
the other contribution (Black bicycles are
double the cost of Halfords red/white girls
bicycles).   //Extracts from my diary, thought you might
                                                    be interested//
Tues. 26.12.06 I saw @ 9.10 A.M. Four Magpies this
morning. One walked accross the road to my (119)
front door and then perched on Eve of house (6'away)
Beautiful slim body. Blue patch on centre of back?
Black body and white under belly. Very elegant
walk :— Purposeful and elegant. Two of them
courted opposite on roof tops wagging
tail signals of love to each other.

                                    R.E.O.

1st January 2007. Wonderful weather, wonderful day. Black birds and sea gulls flying everywhere! At (D) (dead) Virginia ~~creeper~~ pulled down (overgrown). At Breakfast (119) Two robins flew off the ground and kissed.

Love as always.

Jid

25⅜. 2007

119th Heathrow Inn
Great South West Rd.,
Hounslow

Dear Shayla,   Sunday afternoon,
I'm so glad I saw you and
Daniel, yesterday. Enclosed is another
2nd Class stamp (23p). No table so I write
on my overnight bag (suitcase), with a
Paris Hilton pen (made of recycled
paper & looks ~~high~~ like a Banger
(firework).
                    concerned
   A little ~~worried~~ about your young
rottwiller (as you and Daniel were
bitten by a large dog above Guildford
Cathedral (I took you for a long walk
over fields (bare) shooting one arrow
with a young man's Bow. I dare say
you and Daniel have forgotten.
   The field at the end of the

20

three, had very long dark green grass (wild), where there are a number of metal seats. Your hand was nipped by a dog, because you stopped in total fear, I shouted at you both to "come on" in vain (initially). I enclose some "funnies" (Kids Corner). Managed to do a wash today, the machine is noisy and has been in constant use since Thursday. I share an Inn with seven others, (All nationalities). Very friendly. Still painful legs and have to live from moment to moment, as I am incredibly forgetful. Dissapline is a good friend at the moment. Very busy Monday, Docs, specialist (TOES). Clean & tidy house, except Lithuanian woman love fried food, so air is "greasy". Not too sure about future. But HOPE for true love to show her face with wisdom. Hugs and Kisses to my children x DAD x x

Saturday 26th May 2007

A
Kestral
West Middlesex Hospital
'Isleworth'

Dearest Shayla,

I am so glad you answered your mobile yesterday.
Lovely hot weather here, possible rain Sunday.
I would love to hear about your activities on your
Spanish holiday. Perhaps you could write a tale of joy
with your imagination, about where you are staying, some
beauty spot, or elaborate on a particular event.
Before I talked to you (18.46p.m. Friday) I popped into Syon Park
and rode around the grounds. If you remember (No.1) the
estate house is on the right and a couple of lovers were hiding
their horseplay in the deep recess (moat) before the black iron gates
main entrance. Remembering the Butterfly house, I just cycled
around three dolphins, which formed a waterfountain.
Going back to the main drive of the grounds, there is a
magnificent strip (6 feet wide) of wild blue flowers (passion?)
which extends the full length of two fields, before the B.H. and carpark.
(To bring you up to speed, feel free, to swap letters with your
brother). The land including two modern outbarns have been leveled,
this is to make way for a large Hotel! (not connected
directly to S.P.) I also discovered that the railway (miniature)
in the S.P.'s garden was removed two years ago, apparently sparks
were being emitted from the train's wheels with such regularity that they blackened the grass
Lastly, I saw in passing, a wedding banquett in the house's
conservatory/ come round domed greenhouse all with posh black bald
security man!
   As I told Daniel I now have my personal property 'on site'
and I must now exercise my legs for a top up on both mobly
and wallet.
   There is a nice garden here, with small shrubbs & short
slender trees, Lots of sitting & talking. It measures (40' x 200'?)

22

sufficient food always, not as good as fresh, if you know
what I mean?

Very mixed bag of people (20), some mouth-off, some are "loud,"
but most are thoughtful.

There is also a small tributary, meandering waterway,
frequented by squirrels, and pigeons. It is at the base of the
slope, down to the waters edge that two large trees are growing
one an oak, the other a weeping willow, whose branches, having
grown extensively, now submerge the tips of their hanging branches
under water. (P.S. They have now left the water (come out)!!

I have seen a number of unusual mallards (black and white
markings).

I have decided to stay on (see Daniel's letter) until my legs are
better. Sometimes I could do with some help, but I manage
generally sitting down in shops or banks, due to this painful
ill at ease state I have been in for over three years.

Still useless at computer instructions, and I am just resting
until I can become "all fired up" and ready to move again, with
ease.

Missed alot of appointments, in the past (14/5, 15/5, 16/5, 17/5)
ranging from Doc. appoint. meditation course, probation reports, and
further court cases.

With all the turmoil of hospital interviews assessments,
and solicitor instructions, alot of activities have been missed
in the two weeks I have been here.

Hope your flight was good and no delays?

It would be good if you noted in a diary, day to day,
living events. Please remember to tell me all about the
natural beauty of Spain's natural wildlife, especially birds.

P.S. Seen lots of mating pigeons, swallows, high up in numbers,
and three green and yellow parrots! Love from Dad xx

23

Sunday 8/7/07

Dear Shayla,

Good to see you and Daniel yesterday
Never mind about the Lamar — forgive bad writing,
but it is done on my knee whilst sitting on
grass by some water below Paris H, Heathrow.
After "Hello" purchase I cycled on tow-path
to Staines. As I reached Penton Hook
lock, I discovered my mobile was not in
my pocket (PANIC) Returned to the Lamas
Lalekem, but could not find it on the grass.
Alot of people remained drinking with the
        all sitting
bar maids, at the tables, indoors by the
pavilion. A man "called" my number,
but I heard no ring (on the grass!)

returned to Dolphin's, to no avail. Shop was
last checking point, but now 6.15 pm it was shut.
Then cycled to Ashford for a change (to
catch the train "home.") Could not buy ticket
again, so stopped off at Feltham. Felt
hungry (non 7pm ish) N.B. (Seagulls) flying
here overhead & squaking (crying out), as I
write to you! Bought old sandwich &
banana at station. Ticket office was
closed (for a break). (Glad to hear
Ashford High, that was, is changing for the
better)). Decided to cycle all the way
back to Isleworth. Slept well (& today
midday 2 hours). So will continue tale
on Daniel's letter. —

P.S. You left your (my) presents at ⓓ
(Granny's).

Love Dad ✗

8th July 2007,

Dear Daniel,

Still sitting on the grass in the fresh
air! Yesterday, I left Isleworth 10 a.m
by train (with bicycle). Paid for ticket to
Weybridge by mistake (from train ticket man
(on board train). Asked for £1. refund but he
was too busy fining girl with wrong ticket
(£20 fine!) Girl gave me £1 !!! So I did
not have to wait, cycled to Get Fosters for a
coke & then Egham for Lasagne, had a
coke whilst looking at (Thorpe Park) fun Fair
(at the back of the carpark) before stopping
off for a five minute watch of a cricket
match on the green at Chertsey.

Peter

Dropped into my fav. Young's pub for a
swift ½ pt. shandy, Then I came
down the river road to Laleham Park,
and Tel. Shazli at 2. p.m.
So glad you are both very busy
enjoying life.

Love Dad.
P sirel.

Thursday 6.45 pm PM

29 Windsor Road
Sunbury on Thames
Middlesex. TW16 7DY
25th October 2007

Dearest Son,

  Left my keys in bedroom door, had to (4 pm.) wait 1½ hrs. for Billy (the other tenant) to let me in. Catalogue of disaster moves on my part. Went food shopping Tesco, seemed to take hours. Had two hours left of the day so left with too much extra shopping to do in Stamies/xmas (& myself (soap roll-on top up)). Stood for 10 minutes by locked up bicycle shed, could not move (hung over water barrel frozen in pain). (LEGS) Then discovered no keys for bicycle shed (I had left them in my bedroom door lock! Hopeless. I telephoned three people but to no avail. It's hard to carry on loving life, where reduced to sitting in a porch (at least out of the wind & drizel). Mark (another tenant) who is the Landlord could not come out until 7.30 pm. So small mercy

talked to a man (90 yr old) on merchant ships carrying stores of grandchildren by this train in this FOUR children's seaman who the last war, he now has many

I was let in.

I'm about 14½ stone so am trying to eat smaller meals to loose weight.

Plenty of exercise, (as you must realise) with the bicycle. (Auto Ⓓ olphins.

Changed oil yesterday, I was in two minds, whether to bother or not, but it has been 18 months, so thought best to.

Shayla has told me she wants a digital camera, what would you like for Christmas 2007?

I hope to see you, if you can spare the time, at Xmas? I have always missed being there with you all, and pray that God will protect you in this evil world of contradictions and hypocrasies. Always stand up for the truth, I was weak at 21 and let the establishment crusify me. As you well know I love women, and all peoples, but perhaps not knowing llove, as it is, I ask that you will come to know how wonderful a world this creation is.

Yours in Christ,
love you,   Dad (Nigel)

1.03AM. Daniel, 7th December 2007,
    Perhaps you hate me to death,
still I love you. Though many
wish me harm, reject me
outright. Bitter with resentment
and misunderstanding, still I love you,
Never being hugged by you is
a tradgedy, I forgive you.
Remember I have been with you
from the beginning. Never stop
loving your sister and mother
that Bond you cannot ~~bake~~ break.
You are a beautiful person
no-one can change that.
    May the peace of God be upon
you now and guide you in
your life. I enjoyed my youth
the best. Love as always, your
father Nigel.

Shayla on(BIKe) Popped into ST.
2Smiths (No more fancy
writing paper (Sea gulls
and country Stiles)).
Took my baby pack
of Crayons (to ST. &
Back to Knotcutts)
to draw Knibbles
Lookalike & Fred
below.
Perhaps you could
send me (or give later)
the Argos Catalogue Nᵒ for your frame.
*I would like Daniel to ask me for something
for future use (practical) in his life.

N.B. There was a miniture tribe of
three mice(?) you would have loved
and the multitude of birds noises
kept me company, whilst I
sketched the guinea pigs!

Missed the last two Barbee's
but not ²day (FRI 7/8).
Hope you are OK. & having fun.
I never told you about my early
life (I could not settle in any

jobs from 20 - 30 years of age, and I had as many (15) jobs in those few years!

My first job was with Sainsbury's in Walton -on-Thames. I was always late (8.30 A.M. start) so only lasted a few days.

During my tennis days (Weybridge) in the 1970's I cycled to a Saturday job in Kingston-on-Thames (Bentall's food Hall). That was quite good fun.

Anyway dear, love to my fish, or is that another story? TRUE STORY! On (13th) July 2009, late Ev, I overheard this wooshing noise. So I removed my cotton wool from my two ears and opened the outside door; the apparent noise was motorway traffic (M3 ?²⁵) . An adult frog was sitting facing me. I took a short intake of breath in shock! On (17th) July 2009, I found a baby frog under the ~~the~~ outside door bottom base (but WITHIN the door frame!!!) in a corner! I enclose some fragile meltables (pre-chilled in fridge) and spicy (mexican cheddar) cheese. ENJOY, PLease NOTE One of choc Bouchée Côte D'or IS FOR DANIEL. Sleep Well Love & Happy Days ahead xx Love Dad, H&K xx

PS- Suck the buttons, one, evenings,

How are you coping with this heat wave? Ended up _____ in Quagmire mid-day to day. Surrounded by horses with covers over their eyes!

Tuesday night. Strange, Girl

My lonely Boy.   a

I'm glad I bonded with you, "steam-rollering" the living-room carpet together.
     You and Daniel's childhood years were wonderful. I guess I wasted a lot of time on my own in the garden, weeding and time of cars. I saved money then and all through my life, since the age of 21, when I put £52 aside each year in a wealth maker (I told card if I died she would get 52K) Still all that's gone, on court fees and settlements (14K), (10K was the wealth maker policy with Commercial Union) I am still in a strange life of uncertainties, and yes I am seeking to occupy the rest of my life, with a positive outlook, Thank You for asking. It looks as though I will be beginning some beneficial life, but no specifics yet.

Time, again, has cheated our closeness and the years I have lost with you all, are not and never will be, my choice.

As I told Daniel, in his letter, I adored family life, and the closeness, even though I know I should have made more effort, to be with you all, more often. As you know, I was always exhausted with work, and being careful with money created an unnecessary barrier with priorities. Naturally holidays, and day trips, out, suffered, but I am sure you know my love for my family will always be exist, even though I feel dead inside. Never forget, that you are loved, whatever happens to me, and that you are both cherished by your heavenly father above, I will never forget that family matters, and life without love is futile, I'm so happy you have found good friends. Please make sure you are always No. 1.

love forever, your earthly father, Nigel A?

How are you coping with this heat wave?
Ended up in a quag mire!
mid-day   today,
Surrounded   by horses with covers
over their   eyes! strange

My Lonely Boy, α   Tuesday night

I want to remember you as a little boy
I took for granted. I wish I could have bonded
and held you in my arms. I can't remember
when I last hugged you. I was always too busy
with work, house, garden or car, If I had one
wish, it would be a chance to give you one
embrace, I have been too hard on everybody and
myself. I did not know any better. I know that
tenderness and soft touching heals, I have
always wanted to have a life time of
friendship and love, I tryed, but not hard
enough, A loving father should come naturaly
and for some reason I wanted to save money, for the
future for all of us. I never tryed to go away
for ever, but I guess its difficult to tell you
how it is now, Nothing brought me as much

happiness, as home life, I am not as strong as your mother, just different. We all try and survive, but I believe love is more important than telly and food. If god has a plan, it is always with love. His friendship lasts a lifetime and beyond. I want you to Bond more with Shayla, you should both learn to help each other, I have never stopped giving, and helping others. Try to love everybody, but remember to look after No.1. (yourself) first. I'm glad I had fun with you in the bath at No.9, and Carol in her striped T-shirt. We should have washed and cared for each other ALL the time, and told each other our hearts desires. I know she loved her hand (palms) tickled, and I adored her touch on my arms' and back. (A true siberite!) Caring is a vital ingredient in personal relationships, Loyalty is a gift given if trust is honoured, I enjoyed and reveled in responsibility. Something I was not given in spades at both schools, Probably because I was always surviving bullies, I had little inclinations for friendships, but sustained six

from your satisfying Dad Mike, M., and know he always watches over you

God bless you one

six, anyway

36

Dearest Daniel,   Friday
                               4th April 2008 10.52 pm.

    Good to see you on Monday
with Mark, Irene and Hugo (and Emily)
and the other day under those
circumstances' inappropriate!

    Bless you for the helmet. I am
glad you and granny get on well.
I used to with mine (mother's mother)
                    (Neighbour of Mother's, opposite Dolphins)
    Talked to Roz, because brick wall
has descended over access, and I had
to offer the single bed and chair I
had left behind at 29, W/R, so-T. (1k
total), but she says no. Pity really,
because the base of the bed in my
old room, is broken.

37

At least I tried to give 'her indoors' something back.

Glad I heard, in conversation, that you are enjoying Uni. I hope your work goes well, love.

Could not eat (proper food) last night, as I did not have a cooker (only 'micro wave) — and the pastie I cooked was burnt to a frazel. Luckily there was a hob, so I had some pasta', a little bland (I had no cheese!)

Hope you enjoyed your Easter break at home.

God bless you son, always.

Love as ever, Dad x.

N.B. Still have not seen the coast for two years!!

Friday Evening (late)

Dearest Shayla love, Friday 4th April '08,
Good to hear your voice after this
Easter break, Life is hard at the
moment, my own doing, as usual.
I was quite active the three days
before "my off" exit from Sudbury X.
Saw the film 10,000 years B.C., on
Saturday night (11 pm finish!) at a
cinema in Feltham. Sorry about
our brief contact at Grays on
Monday, I regretted not staying
with you THAT was inappropriate.
Played badminton on the Tuesday
at Staines (afternoon) 3rd time lucky.
(I originally turned up the 1st time on
the wrong day, and in the second
attempt, I turned up too late, Nevermind)

Wednesday, I used a free voucher (Informed) to attend my one hour swim at Sunbury Leisure Centre (Informed). Spent 3 hours on ~~Thursday~~ Wednesday packing up from 29, Windsor Road. Apparent upset with voting, Council Tax, and Bus pass dr closure of information. Oh well that's Life! S. & then Ev. again from ② (Gran's). B Stayed here before (4 years ago), seems I have started all over!

How is school? DO WRITE (please) to me. ℅ Dolphins, & I hope to see you again very soon. Had my first drive in a manual learner vehicle, in 18 years, on Thursday (P.M.) Quite a shock! I was told off for coasting (when the clutch is depressed) (around corner (turning left)) Friday 4/4/08 I cycled to Staines Job Centre, but have mislaid C.V. Do give my love to Daniel, Before I left 29, W/R SOT I remembered that I ~~said~~ talked about a rabbit (seeing your "RABBIT" card), and the wire netting that still remains in Heston (Nippon Express), MAYBE ONE DAY DARLING LOVE &

Enclosed is your guarantee (receipt) for the camera, as always, kisses as

& keep asking in shops for employment. I have to look for myself, Darling. & remember about looking & listening on the road (safety 1st)

'Dearest Shay'n   Sunday afternoon 18/6/00,
    Finally seeing a misty green triangular light I feel inspired to thank you for a lovely father's day. Love the velvety choc. T.
    Please write an account of your next weekend (afterwards, of course!) & send it to (me) % Dolphins, Blacksmith's Lane.
    Do check up on the highway code for your bicycle. I'm not very good at wearing my helmet either, but perhaps it would be wisest in WET weather! (not bullying you)!
    Forgot to mention the rabbits at the end of the garden, have not totally disappeared. I saw a single baby sitting on a patch of grass, beyond the end of 31, Cromwell Grove, Shepperton's (P.T.O.

2 garden fence; not two feet from my face! and obviously dazed by the heat of (Friday) because it refused to move from the shade of a large Dandelion weed, leaf, fell asleep again, watching some fantastic tennis, having put the bicycle rack away in their garage and swallowed ½ pint of guinness (a bit of a heavy bitter. I don't think you would like it!)

I hope you have a lovely time next week in the new forest, camping.

I am a little worried about Daniel and I. He did not cash his Xmas cheque, and I have not given him anything for his Birthday. Perhaps you could talk to him. Do share this letter if you wish.

Love from Dad & andalong

Glad we both relaxed on that mound, after our picnic (Bedfont Lakes.)

P.S. What is Daniel's new Address?

(AR. Shepperton Studios)
Sunday 15th June 2008,

Dear Son,

Life is very hard at the moment.
I have inherited my father's high blood
pressure, and the drugs I am meant to
be taking are making my ankles swell up
like balloons!

It is also unfortunate that I have gained
4 stone, so carrying around this extra dead
weight is quite wearying.

Finally decided to press on with the
old motor, and pay an extortionate £606
for my road sins (insurance)

Shayla kindly "took" me out to
Bedfont Lakes for some lunch & cycle ride,

43

I am still quite jaded from a cycle trip to Hampton Court, the other day.

I use my bicycle whenever I can in an effort to stay fit and loose some more 'baggage!' also I am eating more sensibly and _Less_ food.

The three burning issues in my life are amalgamating :- Job, house & love life.

Glad you have found a house to share, enjoy your parties - I am green with envy.

Love always,

Dad.   (Nigel.)

313,

Raining, Saturday. 7.10 p.m.

Naughty Shayla! who loses my address,
promises to write (last month), was
going to see me, but starts with a
boot sale! but hey, who's
complaining. NOT ME.
I still love you,
Must tell you about my wonderful
savings at my local charity shop.
Firstly, the (one) pair of trousers
(jeans) I can wear had become
so dirty (soiled) they desperately
needed a wash, but I could not
wear my shorts either as my
waist is too big! So I tullied myself

45

into going to Shepperton.

Then my Doc. told me to go to the Gym, but I had no shorts to wear. So guess what? Yes, that's right, I paid another visit to C/S. shop.

The trousers & shorts I picked up were very reasonable (10% of normal prices!!) You never know what you might find — why don't you have a look yourself one day, love.

Ran my food stocks right down this week, so had to (circumstances) shop early (9am—10am) Tesco.

Still have [not] got Daniel's *forwarding address*. Please ASK mum (yours) to pass it on to me via my mother. Ta. (Again))

Here's a short poem (which a Co. wanted to publish (but I had to pay/£) so to put it into a composition book

27.6.2008 3pm

I shall sit down
Tell you stories of old,
How hard a life
and death untold,
Staggered battles
that tear the soul,
And kind hearts
will heal a coming touch.

Simon and your friends
with swords of flame
Remember love,
a treasured game.
Be still I say,
One day I'll come
and set you free
A challenge to be.

Love
you
always
Dad xx
Babe.

B & B
Shepperton

Daniel,

Saturday 1st ~~June~~ November 2008,

Last Friday (24/10) I made myself walk a good two miles through orange & red "tunnels" of trees to Mickleham Downs. It was a brand new walk and five horses came by from their field into the wooded area by the path fence (I said Hello to them) on my return journey.

I cannot find my 2nd pair of Long Johns, so washed 1st as my legs were beginning to itch. Notice how cold it is generally, so heating goes on quite regularly. (Kitchen has no door, so the hall, and it, are one). Be wise with warmth, I am sure I do not have to remind you about the time you ended up in hospital, love.

I saw a one bedroom flat, but it would be too much of a drain on resources (3K). Still trying to find part-time work, so at least you can have some pin money for Christmas and on.

I continue with ~~counselling~~ Thurs.room. and Tues. if my positive course. Be

Replaced 5 light bulbs, finally (bought months ago).

at Mother's. She prized the information out of me, as usual, and then tried to feed me with ice-cream! (Energy saving lights)

It would be good to see you again this Christmas, if you can spare the time. (Know your granny (my mother) enjoys is always thrilled to see you and Shayla.

Saw Shayla two weeks in a row!! 19/10 and 26/10. We cooked some chicken breasts, with jacket potatoes + greens. On the second Sunday Shayla prepared the whole meal of mince, ginger, onions, and red pepper, mustard, tomatoes (tinned), garlic and spagheti.

Are not the deep blue nights fabulous, all those stars.

Wanted to try and give a large rabbit to Shayla for Xmas, which I know she wanted, but everyone is afraid of the dogs! So no.

Although I have played Badminton regularly, I am still overweight, and fitness eludes me.

Started a healthier 'diet' (better food consumption) with a little help from a fitness expert (written good food lists).

Keep your good work up, and enjoy your free time, I'm sure you do anyway love Bisa man & xxx

31

Beloved Daniel,   1ˢᵗ December 2008,
    The rabbits are jumping around
in the overgrowth today and lots
of flying activity as usual.
    I will keep trying to get employment.
    There is so much deception and
lies. I love women but I cannot
trust.
    A friend tried to stay with me
(request) but I told her I live in
a B & B and could not even give
her a nest from her persecuting
son.
    There is an enormous dog who

49

is wonderfully loving. I stroked
its head and scratched its back,
in the hallway, at the old pig farm,
as I paid my weekly rent and
handed over my clothes for their
kind washing favour. How do you cope?
Is there an internal machine, or
do you have to "walk the streets"?
  The cats seem to love me too.

  Fantastic weather; Glorious day
I sat in the sun for a moment
and listened to favourite tunes
on the radio.
  I am not well and have
started chanting and raving.
  Never mind. Too much on my
own.
  Banned two weeks; lost it at
badminton... stood up for myself
verbally. so have suffered a small
setback. (over now) God be with you

always. love from your father xxxoxxxoo

P.S. Please forgive my weak drive, I feel I let you down with the ice-skating. Have tried to ring you many times.

Lovely Shayla<, Thurs. 1st January 2009,

If you find this letter wobbly, it is because I am writing on last years calendar 2008 you gave me! Just finished letter to Daniel, which I enclose for you to give him, please.

My intentions are still honourable, and I will not give up the fight for life.

As you know (please feel free to read Daniel's letter) life is a pain in the neck (which is also stiff)

Please behave with that teacher of yours (past trouble, remember being banned? (suspended)

Good to see Elton John, momentarily (on the box) belting out "Philadelphia Freedom", (it was the 1st single record, I ever bought).

51

submitted a couple of drawings to Alison (our local priest). They are for a (logo) design amalgamation (two local groups).

Must fix my glasses (they keep falling off my nose!) tomorrow.

Travelled back to (D) garage to pick up my 'footprint' screwdriver AGAIN! pain, never mind. Must bleed my radiator (top 25% is stone cold) of air. The bleed bolt does not have a head, but a slot (for a screwdriver) My new year's moto is 'TRY TO BE ASSERTIVE EARNEST AND HONEST! I will miss my 7½K view (eventually) my lovely Robin squirrels, cats, and grey rabbits one day but not the noise of the boiler and power shower. Long Johns was going to be my Xmas request, but at £15, a little bit expensive — never mind. I found my missing pair, anyway! Love from Daddy

Let's do something constructive and

(right margin, rotated) (GREENS and FRUIT) enjoy!!! and eat well, keep WARM. Productive.

Beloved children be kind & gentle.

1st January 2009,

Dear Daniel,   Still in Shepperton,

Thank you for Christmas Boxing day,
It was good to see you in such high
Spirits, especially masterminding
family fortunes, I enclose (copy of) a card
you and Shayla sent me many (lovely) moons ago,

Betrayed by my aquaintaces New
Year's eve, but survived. Hope you had
fun,

You never asked how I spent my
Christmas day and your news was
rather spartan,

U must realies by now I
cannot forget the horror of the

53

last four years.

I still try to smile and
progress is slow,

One of the women of '2004'
from Staines C. C. office was
doing some charity work and
she told me (reminded) about
the past (on Christmas Day).

When I got home, I decided
(after a full year of itching (Psoriasis))
to cut my hair again (Nº 4), not
alot better, and my back wound
still itches on a regular basis.

Still aim to be positive,

Keep contact with your Granny,
she loves you very much.

I Hope you enjoy your life and we
~~3rd December~~ will meet again,

Mark Teare might come over again soon
Best wishes to your mate & the 3 girls! Dad

22.09 P.P.S. 4.30AM   * Shipperton Studios (No.9) sun x.
Do not forget snow ball fights!? Just had to step outside
barefoot in the snow
(leave an impression;
(footprint in the snow
I was here!)). *

Dear Daniel,   1st February 2009,
Continuing on from Shayla's letter
of 1.2.09. I stopped off after my services
and lunch, in Feltham, as it was still
early (3.30 p.m). I have not socialized
in a number of days, and naturally go a
little unhinged. Have been asked to
re locate, and requested by another
to help out as a groundsman, said no
because it is such a dead end job,

    Still very cold down here in the SE
of London town,

    Hope you are still eating well, at least
at W/Ends.

    I believe one day you will be
able to love someone, who you can

55

trust. It is so important to be able to share your life with someone who cares, and will be able to stand by your side, even in stormy weather.

It is always so sad, to have a one sided relationship. Wisdom seems to come at a heavy price.

The birds are quite tame today, they hang around the fence, at the bottom of the garden for longer periods of time, and they onto the grass, quite regularly, moreso.

Quite a few B&B engineers have been staying over, the last two weeks. They are servicing the long (and high) rides at Thorpe Park (structure and CHAIN DRIVE management).

Glad you managed to see Granny before you returned to B University.

Love from Dad - a snow man (Usling

P.S. Remember building bits of coal for buttons?
2.2.09. Heavy snow and red sky this morning!)

* Perhaps you could send your correspondence to me % Dolphins, still use my name though.

(overlapping/crossed text - partially legible) ... 7 nights, 2.2.09 2.45 AM ... them couldn't ... up! Motorbike ... to work, spread eagle legs on Richmond Road, going to work — nothing will stop ... us! 4" floor board nail ... because ... U/S £80, Loosing licence, Loosing 1" ... the rush home in Weybridge ... Sunday roast, the old lady St ... airport bike. Dear Shayla ... so many memories ... February 2009. my family everything! By love ... again!! LOVE 2

What a fabulous day today was, I hoped you enjoyed it too.

I spent a while ~~last~~ yesterday evening preparing a meal for a small group of Methodists, today. I also cooked my tea, so I was quite ~~boisterous~~ and mad, with the pressure.

It would be good for you to use your brain & write back to me, occasionally, (Anna, Banana)

*The last time you did was 6th April, 2006.

Just made it to a 9.30 AM Candle ~~Light~~ (hand held) mass at 9.30 AM. this morning, near the airport. Lovely service, about 'the' Light of the world! Always gleam so much encouragement and guidance.

Don't forget Grans B'day etc.!

Started to snow as I arrived on the drive of residence 4.45 pm.

Saw a flock of Canadian geese in the horse field (NR. TIP) and large number of seagulls flew did a 'fly past' my window, followed by three crows, strange 50p text received, M?

Have you ever noticed that Nothing is as it seems. For example; there was a folding prayer rest in the church this morning, it was covered by a plastic material (like Fablon). The rest looked like wood. Only by touching it, did it become apparent that it was soft, and cushioned with foam!

On Wednesdays, I attend a local morning service for an hour. The church has several outer rooms, and when they are locked. To use their loo, I had to ask because the door bolts were invisable (painted black, like the back door to which they were secured) God bless my

As I finished my walk, today, a swan came in to land on the canal ...

Dear Beloved Children,   8th March 2009,

Only four sheets of both countryside and seagulls left – are you glad?!

Missed the sunshine this morning; I laid in, idle. Hope you read my text 'Hi ~ whad U up 2 ?! It's cold here, wear H.M. (planes) LD H & K.' Thought I would help you to deceiffer! H.M. is my Holy Mountain, which looks onto the Hilton Hotel and Heathrow Airport, one side. And on the other side lies a lovely view Rwin as well Two Bridges Farm. It is a large mountain, grassed and is hidden by the dual carriageway with a large sweep of yellow flowers, bedded in a "wave" type pattern (almost a smile shape). On the other side the view encapsulates a canal (waterflood management) and on the far side of the canal bank there roams a young Shirehorse and two foals. The canal is lined with trees and reeds, ducks & moorhens. As I arrived, I saw a duck with a broken wing (sagging), it was still agile and walked quickly away, splashing into the water, as they do. At the top of the mountain there are a number of wild tree type bushes and a perfect grass area for lying down in the sun.

some dog had left its business there, so I flicked it away with a stick, as it was luckily dry. Started to pick up rusty old coke and beer cans. Filled a windswept orange bag with them and found a bin at the far end of a the very well made grey stone (compressed) footpath. It poured with rain as I left 44, and small, white hail stones descended too! 'LDH&K' (to finish off previous page (text)) = Love Dad Hugs Kiss, in case you have forgotten! ∝ Had an idea for a slogan the yesterday! KISS = Keep it simple, Sir !! Daft aye' Loved the sky turning a rich light blue as I walked there this afternoon, (the whole sky was dark and grey when I arrived, just as the rain stopped), but there was a bitterly cold winter wind. Saw a few locals walking their dogs. Oh, I nearly forgot, I popped into Tesco as usual, in a twelve car jam! There was a lady, quite young, who took a good year to make her exit. ((I waited so long for her space, that I caused a traffic jam! As it began to rain again, I had no choice but to get out and get wet! before I could manage to guide her to reverse into the T junction space (she was unsure what to do, poor girl). No problem really, (I just seemed to be waiting forever) - lots of people rudely hooted their horns as they passed by!!! How is your bicycle? Still functioning O.K.? Love to Daniel. I hope you are all well and fit. I have just started on 8 week keep fit course, and swam at Staines pool: my shoulder joints were clicking quite madly. Tried the Sauna too. It was 446°F, hotter than Africa! Love to you Shayla Dad

60

Dear Daniel,   Saturday 20th June 2009,

I had forgotten that my last letters to you
and Shayla were in April.

Hope you enjoyed your B'day card "novelty"
joke (& Earl Grey Tea Leaves.)

I have suffered various setbacks, but obviously
not sharing the last five years with you, and
Shayla, as a family, has been hard.

I keep breathing & try to remain outgoing
and positive.

Now I am at a stage of crossroads.

The hardest part is losing my excess
baggage; I am still fat. Not obeisse, but
shapely "teddy" style.

There have been a number of day trips
to *Brighton and *Bournmouth, including
*Glastonbury and Romsey. I have not been
to Romsey. (I did not revisit the others *)

I hope you will enjoy a break, soon. (after 33 years!)
I joined YHA again, but am still uncommitted, to a holiday.

Drove to Hampton swimming pool, already in trunks & under leggless jeans (cut off to make shorts)

The old fireball automobile is very expensive this year. What a total waste of £more this mess is (too many much "K's" to mention).

Just started to try and put into motion routine and purpose, although both goals are elusive at present.

Just spent the last hour racking my brain about when I visited West Beach. I had circled in green ink (13th April) with absolutely nothing written down in my diary! Anyway, it was then that I drove back accross the estuary to L'Hampton (where we stayed once and I got locked out of the triumph car, and latter had my radio aerial broken off by Vandels, and then again 2 weeks later in Metcalf Road (2 hours to fit new aerial (had to drop pull out the radio & feed the new (aerial) cable by string through the car side panel and through all the electrics of the dash board) Re-call? Swam in a sharp (cold sea). Had Fish & chips in our restaurant fed some swans bread. Drove on to Bognor Regis, and split HAD STRAWBERRY treated myself to clock Golf. Had a larger (½ a pint) then came back

20th April tryed to flog "Oh", but old book shop owner not interested, So had sandwiches in Syon Park & then walked to their huge willow tree, beside the lake. My feet were surrounded by three or four baby ducks. One decided to walk between my legs and then under the wooden seat fixed to the willow tree. Good luck with your exams. Do well, Love Dad.

Clue: Bananas -- ------ Digi (Cap...)
What goes under what?? (4 U & Daniel,
19.8.09 8AM (OBSCURE) Invented Riddle)

(P+P)
(+) = church

Darling Sheyla, Thursday 20th August 2009,

Tryed stretching myself (yesterday) 19th
Stared in water (ST.) very crowded. Enjoyed
having fun with five graduates. Three W.
two M. (all lookers).

TREE 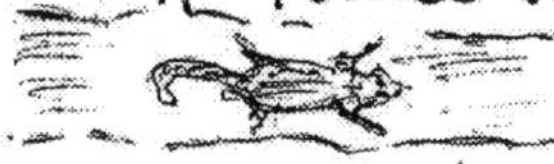

Then two hunks (would have knocked you
out) appeared (with huge V torsos) One had a
light black 'Mowri' tatoo on the whole of his
back (V shaped). The pattern was very similar
to Robbie Williams arm one. Was not too
pleased with the Japenesse crowd (S), as they
were swimming erraticaly and not
clockwise or anti-clockwise in our allotted
two lanes, which we lost to swimming
coaches after ½ hr. (Children's Lessons)
Jaccusy was prohibited by a crusty S/C
who feared collisions, but by now it was
cold & turned off (no empting bubbles)
Received a cut on my bigtoe, at the baths —

GATES 

HAD TWO 19th VISITS from Squirral (S?) — don't know how!

very cross SWAN (ST.) moving at 5 m.p.h. +

W/Ev.

~~Nigel to~~ Called you many times, you should know by now what I do not like (A/M). ~~Hope to see you soon.~~ Big day tomorrow, I imagine ~~another & your~~ you all ~~happy~~ celebrating, I Always have my outside door open : as you know I love fresh air.

You may find this hard to believe, but we (all) change quite dramatically. ~~when~~ It is almost a total ~~total~~ reversal. ~~activity,~~ I am so glad that you have found school fruitful.

I wish you good results,

You have yet to give me information previously requested (7+/8)

I saw two Doberman ~~with~~ their owner, as I cut across the park to ✝ for exercise last Wednesday. ~~It foward~~ ~~was still in Hot, but I was too bladey anyway~~ PS. My Uncle David (gone) had three lean enormous dobermans on his dairy farm, I still swat the occasional fly, wasps and flees are

also Prevalent, Be Good, Share & help other persons) always Paul

Particularly the difficult, Love

COVER NOTE FOR LETTERS
The song line which includes "Negotiate the truth",
encapsulates my catch 22.
The fabric of our society is interwoven,
so tightly, with the main professions.
Robbery is a knaves tool,
subtle as Satan is.
A dark overwhelming force,
whom I believe the holy spirit overcomes for us.
This testament, however obscure,
illustrates my deep love for my children.
It was compiled because no one has lifted a finger to
help, in the last ten years.
I survive on the love of strangers,
and my faith.

Other works of Interest ;

Oh (a book of prose)

In. Gold <small>Ad Alta</small>   Duet et Mon Droit   AL

PRINCIPIO ERAT VERBUM   Be Frugal   Dark Horse   Thoroughbred   Master
Unbelievable
Please Please Lord Rejoice Oh Dear Paul A life of Denighal. Just passing through. The
Secret. The Gift. The Kiss.
Book of Words Labour of love Then & Now Gem 147 Enter. Sacre Bleau

To the glory of God. The Grace of our Lord Jesus Christ. The fellowship of the Holy
Spirit. Et Spiritus Sanctum
LOVE ALL
TO SEE or NOT TO SEE that is the **ANSWER. N.o.thing   TRY   ASK**
Go where ever you want to   N   Be prepared! A.n.o.n.
                    Wonderful Find   E
                                    S

C'EST LA VIE!   JOKER   SIMBA   CONSEQUENCES
Life is crazy, life is fun, life is meant to be vital.   **Enough is**
                            Enough is Enough

little rose of creepy vine
Pinkness Sweetness so divine   £5.55 (55p to Chicks)
Like a succulent apple-juice $13.31($1.21 to Chicks)
I will love thee.   Distractions   **Nothing has Changed**   Spud
The Go~Likelies, The Loves, The Woodshills all the Marks, Sh-Andy Charlie,
All the girls I loved in my minds eye, For the love of Justice.

25th July 1977

Oh, the mystic air
that we breatheth,-do partake
Fair trees are hanging over
Nodding sleepy heads
which gently rock upon the shoulders
of the yokels who sitteth on the stools
likened unto the barley malt wheat 'n all
swaying snake ~ waves o'er the red earth.

took me to the T ~ junction (he was going to Arundel).
It was about 6.55 p.m. and I was unsuccessful with the
hitch~hiking. I thought as I started walking that I
might have to sleep it rough. I had walked about 1400
yards, when at 7.30 p.m. a mini stopped. There was a
young girl driving who looked about 19, but she could
have been 20. (I had another fag whilst walking). Her
name was Carol and we talked most of the way. It was
7.45 p.m. when I reached the white gates.   (Fin)

6th December 1971

I came 48th in the Intermediate cross country run,
which Adare won.

N.B. Everything in this autobiography is true.
From 5th June 1972 Calvit was my fag! ~He was
fired on 8th June 1972 for not making my bed for
ages & getting me a P.D.(prefect's detention : lines)
by leaving my tennis shorts to soak in a basin overnight!

4th July 1972

The leaver's dinner was a great success, and the
food was excellent, as well as the red wine. I got a
bit drunk, not to mention the rum & Triple A!!!

SHEET 🎼 usi 🎵

27th June 2008 3 p.m.

Shall I sit down
tell you stories of old ?
How hard a life and death unfold.
Staggered battles that tear the soul
And kind hearts heal
a caring touch.
Surround your fires
with swords of flame
Remember love,
a treasured game.

Be still I say
One day I'll come
and set you free
A challenge to be.

LET THERE BE

Of (a fresh new look)

Gloriously Bright

Some diamonds caught my eye

A glance up to the V gap in the curtains

The heavy rain had dissipated

Hard rain drops remained on the window